Let Me Try!
Hidden Pictures
Preschool Fun Book

Bats swoop high and low. Help them find the
missing tent, mitten, heart, cactus and letter "B".

Please visit us at http://www.waldmanbooks.com.

Printed in the United States of America

TO THE PARENT

Each page in this book has several familiar objects hidden within the artwork. Using the list printed beneath the picture, children find and identify the hidden objects. This fun and challenging activity will increase your child's powers of observation and awareness, and at the same time will give your child a sense of accomplishment and pride as more and more hidden pictures are identified.

This book is especially designed so that the child can use it alone, or with a parent or friend.

The artwork has been created with big, bold lines to make finding the hidden pictures easier for preschoolers. We think your child will have hours of fun finding the hidden pictures, and, as an added bonus, the pictures can be colored!

"Let Me Try!" That's what every child wants to do. HIDDEN PICTURES will enable your child to try — and succeed!

The pig is taking a mud bath. Help him find the
mug, wrench, vase, and **watermelon slice**.

Out for a swim. Help the mother duck and her babies
find the **crown**, **hot dog**, **cane**, **belt** and **cupcake**.

Ken is off to school. Help him find the **lollipop, drum, dog bone, kite** and **hot dog**.

Soccer time. Can you help Rachel find the **bird, bowling pin, rocket, chicken drumstick** and **pair of pants**?

The playful kittens are trying to find the **spatula, flag, stocking hat, broom** and **bunch of grapes** hidden here.

Santa's come and gone. But he left **5 gifts**.
Can you find them?

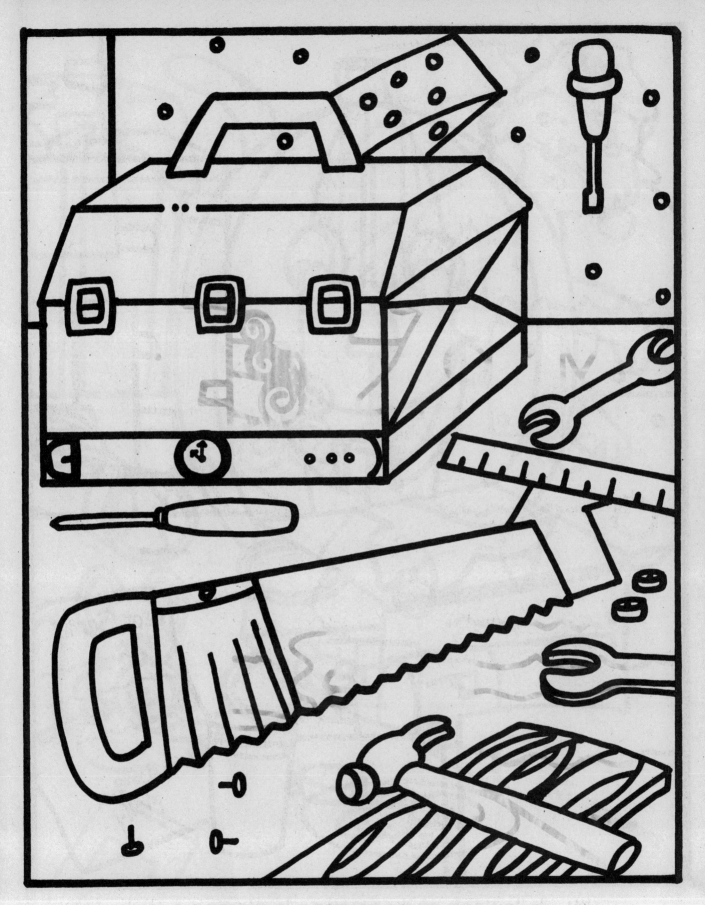

Dad's tool bench is a mess.
Find the **watch, cheese, arrow, envelope** and **skirt**.

It's Halloween and someone is playing a trick.
Can you spot the **tennis ball, bat,
paintbrush, umbrella** and **mailbox**?

10

The seashore has lots of things to see.
But wait! What are the **acorn, frying pan, teapot, mushroom** and **golf club** doing there?

11

Trick or Treat! Can you find the **plate, thermometer, broom, elephant's head** and **cotton candy**?

The book worm. Help him find the **hockey stick,
candle, telescope, sock** and **door!**

13

Do you think the busy butterflies see the **apple slice**, **dress**, **eye**, **funnel** and **snow cone**?

It's time to play hide and seek! Look closely and spot
a **flower, iron, fan, bow** and **pitchfork**.

Puppet play. Can you find the **mushroom, kite, carrot, flowerpot** and **flashlight**?

A swinging time. Can you find a **lemon,**
pliers, frying pan, and **bowling pin**?

Candy store quiz. Can you find the **paint brush,
worm, tulip, dumbbell** and **magnifying glass**?

What a great tree house Allison has! But there's also an **egg, pretzel, suitcase, jump rope** and **bat** here, too!

There's nothing like a cool ice cream treat on a hot day.
If you can find the **five ice cream treats,**
they're yours!

Quick—find the **five hidden caterpillars** before
they eat all the leaves on this plant.

Angela has come to the garden to pick tomatoes.
Can you show her where she'll find **five**?

Breakfast is almost ready.
Before you dig in, find **five missing muffins.**

Here is Samantha's snowman. Can you also find
the **shirt, sailboat, funnel, lightning bolt**, and **light bulb**?

Help Tony find the **teacup, arrow, book, fish** and **bell**.

We're at the zoo! But look, can you also find the
**toothpaste tube, acorn, pair of pants,
chicken drumstick** and **horseshoe**?

The bunny family watches a sunset. It's up to you to find the missing **telescope, watermelon slice, frog, baseball glove and flute!**

Bats swoop high and low. Help them find the
missing **tent, mitten, heart, cactus** and **letter "B"**.

Here's a beary nice picture! Do you see the **crown,
crayon, slice of bread, hamburger** and **apple**?

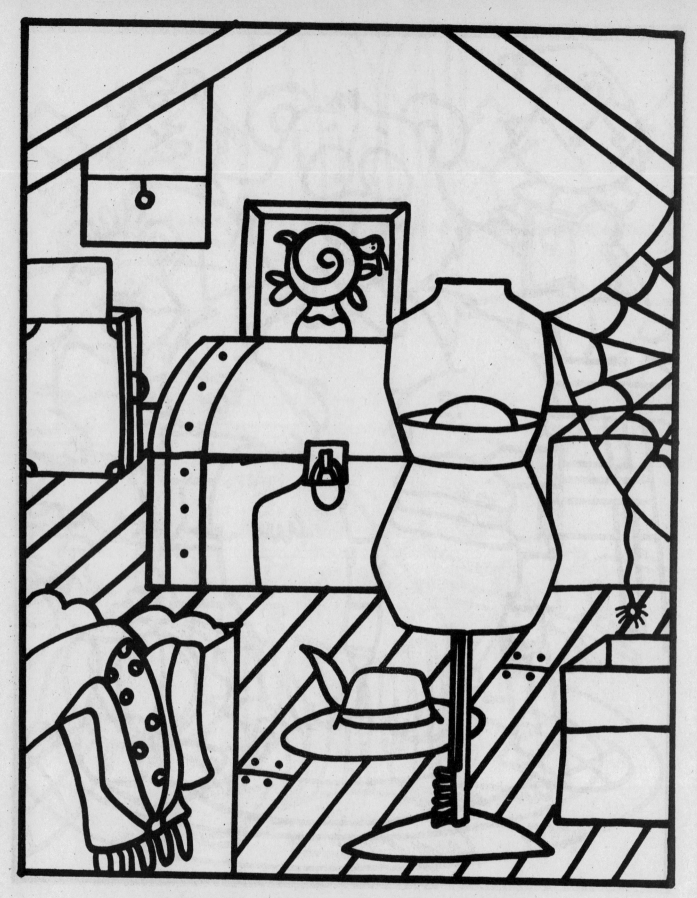

Attic search. Can you find the **snail, sailor hat, boot, toothbrush** and **corn**?

Beavers love to munch on trees.
Can you show them where the **inline skate,**
lizard, rabbit, pumpkin and **saw** are?

The animal friends are busy jumping rope. They have no idea that a **rainbow, pail, glove, balloon** and **boat** are close by!

There's always something to do at the playground.
But have you ever hunted for a **hose**, **camera**, **shovel**,
shell, and **basket** when you're there?

Caroline Kitty just found a giant squash.
Can you help her find the **envelope, baby bottle, baseball, ladybug,** and **ring**?

Wendy Witch wants some new things for her brew.
Help her find a **ghost, bird's head, pea pod,**
ruler and the **number 8**.

Bunny's at the plate. Before he swings, find
the hidden **clothes hanger, piece of cake,
button** and **dog bone** and **moon**.

There are five things hidden in this yummy scene.
Look for the **lock, skateboard, cheese, bowl** and **funnel**.

Brent is painting. But he can't find the hidden
saw, pencil, star, gumdrop and **umbrella**. Can you?

Build a sand castle at the beach. But before you do, find the flipper, toothbrush, the letter W, hat and piece of pie!

The apple pies smell terrific. But can you also find
the **comb, chef hat, heart, key** and **turtle**?

Father bird is chirping away because he found the hidden **ice-cream scoop, lamp, fork, door** and **slice of pizza**.

What is special in the pet shop? A **window, bowling ball, sombrero, watering can** and **cherry**. Can you find them?

Edgar Elephant sees five moons. Do you?

Edwina Elf's job is to wrap gifts. Your job is to find the **bell, dog bone, candy cane, net** and **bowl**!

Ethan Elf is in charge of building dolls. You're in charge of finding the hidden **airplane, shamrock, suitcase, caterpillar** and **glass**.

Do you think the little bear notices the **bow, snake, top hat, ice-cream cone** and **candle**?

Fredrico is trying his new racing car set.
Race to see how fast you can find the hidden
can, scarf, lock, lampshade and **snake**!

Help the lucky leprechaun find the hidden **cap**,
sock, **pickle**, **seal** and **telephone receiver**.

Help baby find her missing things! Look for the **bottle**, **pacifier**, **doll**, **toy radio** and **rattle**.

The circus has hidden surprises. Look close to find
the **bell**, **fish**, **slice of bread**, **wrench** and **drum**.

Sleepy lion cubs are too tired to find the hidden
teacup, radish, nail, feather and **pen.**

The Martians are loading the spaceship. Help them find the **butterfly, zipper, ice-cream cone, duck** and **acorn**.

Hidden in and near the toy chest are a **sailboat, musical note, ruler, baton,** and **clown hat**. Can you find them?

Here's Aunt Sally's sewing room.
Can you find the **ladle, candle,** and **book**?

Melvin Mouse is cooking his dinner. Can you find the hidden **tomato, hammer, beach ball, swan** and **horn**?

Sidney Squirrel is out looking for acorns.
Tell him also to look for the **feather, balloon,
oven mitt, tent** and **piece of candy!**

Mary Mermaid is finding all sorts of things.
Can you help her find a **pair of eyeglasses, banana, orange slice, candy cane,** and **dogdish**?

What a happy hive. Can you find the **spoon,
eye, glass, thread spool and hat?**

Before the birthday party begins see if you can find the
canoe, letter V, television, necktie and **fish!**

A honey sandwich for this bear. But she doesn't see the
hidden **butterfly, glove, pear, heart and cap**. Do you?

60

It's gym time! It's also time to find the hidden
carrot, stick of gum, shoe, peanut and **spatula!**

There are **5 shy little sea horses** here.
Can you find them?

Scarecrow needs help. Can you help him find **5 birds**?

You can see the helicopter!
But can you spot **5 hot air balloons**?

Show Molly where she can find a teapot, cowboy boot, flashlight, broom and **ice cream treat!**

Lucy Leprechaun is looking for **5 pots of gold**.
Can you show her where they are?

A day at the beach.
Start the fun by finding the **clam, ice-cream treat, door, water can** and **telephone receiver**.

Christmas Candles. But look, there is also a **butterfly, horseshoe, bowl, rainbow** and **flag** to find.

What strange things to find in Mom's jewelry box!
A **can**, a **slice of bread**, **key**, **egg** and **knitting needle**.

Show the new chicks where they can find a **leaf,
sock, scissors, tulip** and the **letter "Z"**!

Help Angie find the **pliers, potato, lamp, sneaker** and **fork!**

Ship ahoy! But can you spot the **mitten, pineapple, apron, cake** and **paint brush** before the voyage is over?

Christmas is coming! Can you find the **orange slice,**
letter "V", feather, pancake flipper and **flower**?

What's for lunch? But what is a **dog dish, lock, cap, pair of scissors,** and **golf club** doing there?

A yummy bowl of fruit. But wait, do you see the **pretzel, duck, heart, cupcake,** and **pair of pants** here too?

Hoop time. But can you find the **bowl, snake, spoon, paint brush** and **ice-cream cone?**

Bunny Ballerinas! Can you help them find the
snow cone, ice-cream scoop, corn, balloon and **arrow?**

Jane doesn't know there are 5 things hidden in her bedroom.
Can you find the **frying pan, bird, pair of shorts,
worm** and **chef's hat?**

78

In the toy room! Can you find a hidden **pencil,
flower pot, fish, snow cone** and **hat**?

Becky loves her new vanity. But she doesn't see the
drum, hat, crayon, arrow and **envelope!**

A puppet show! But what are an **inline skate, rocket, pacifier, funnel** and **necktie** doing there?

Lots to see at the pond. Did you notice the **pickle,
football, glove, musical note** and **cowboy hat?**

SOLUTIONS

page 3

page 4

page 5

page 6

page 7

page 8

83

page 9

page 10

page 11

page 12

page 13

page 14

page 15

page 16

page 17

page 18

page 19

page 20

page 21

page 22

page 23

page 24

page 25

page 26

page 27

page 28

page 29

page 30

page 31

page 32

page 33

page 34

page 35

page 36

page 37

page 38

page 39

page 40

page 41

page 42

page 43

page 44

page 45

page 46

page 47

page 48

page 49

page 50

page 51

page 52

page 53

page 54

page 55

page 56

page 57

page 58

page 59

page 60

page 61

page 62

page 63

page 64

page 65

page 66

page 67

page 68

page 69

page 70

page 71

page 72

page 73

page 74

page 75

page76

page 77

page 78

page 79

page 80

page 81

page 82

C511-12/25827/96